MEXICO
the culture

Bobbie Kalman

A Bobbie Kalman Book

The Lands, Peoples, and Cultures Series

 Crabtree Publishing Company

www.crabtreebooks.com

The Lands, Peoples, and Cultures Series
Created by Bobbie Kalman

For Judy and Norman Reiach and Edwin Deal
who brought me to Nassau

Written by
Bobbie Kalman

Coordinating editor
Ellen Rodger

Editor
Jane Lewis

Contributing editors
Kate Calder
Carrie Gleason

Editors/first edition
Tammy Everts
David Schimpky
Janine Schaub
Lynda Hale

Production coordinator
Rose Gowsell

Design and production
Text Etc.

Separations and film
Quadratone Graphics Ltd.

Printer
Worzalla Publishing Company

Special thanks to: Jürgen Bavoni, Danny Brauer, Monique Denis, DeYoung Museum, Library of Congress, Mexican Government Tourism Office, Marla Misunas, and Laurie Taylor

Photographs
Jürgen Bavoni: p. 21 (bottom), 23 (bottom), 24, 26; Jim Bryant: p. 7 (top), 11 (top), 12 (top); Milt & Joan Mann/ Cameramann Int'l., Ltd.: p. 15 (bottom), 19 (both), 22, 23 (top), 27; Betty Crowell: p. 6 (inset); Nancy Giovanelli: p. 4, 6 (bottom); Hollenbeck Photography: p. 8 (bottom), 10, 12 (middle), 16, 17 (bottom), 21 (top left), 28, 29; Wolfgang Kaehler: title page, 20, 21 (top right, bottom); Bobbie Kalman: p. 14, 17 (top); Danny Lehman/Corbis/Magmaphoto: p. 25; Diane Payton Majumdar: p. 7 (bottom); San Francisco Museum of Modern Art: page 13 *Frieda and Diego Rivera*, 1931, by Frida Kahlo; oil on canvas, 100.01 x 78.75 cm (39 3/8 x 31 inches) Albert M. Bender Collection, Gift of Albert M. Bender; the Selena Foundation: p. 15 (top); Superstock/ Steve Vidler: p. 5; other images by Digital Stock

Every effort has been made to obtain the appropriate credit and full copyright clearance for all images in this book. Any oversights, despite Crabtree's greatest precautions, will be corrected in future editions.

Illustrations
Barbara Bedell: p. 18
Antoinette "Cookie" DeBiasi: p. 9 (bottom)
Scott Mooney: icons, p. 30–31
Bonna Rouse: p. 9 (top)
David Wysotski, Allure Illustrations: back cover

Cover: This Toltec statue stands among the ruins found at the archeological site of Tula, in the Mexican state of Hidalgo.

Title page: The Aztec people have lived in Mexico for hundreds of years. Elaborate, feathered costumes are part of their traditional dress.

Icon: Mayan pyramid

Back cover: The chihuahua is a type of small dog that was once kept by the native peoples of Mexico.

Published by
Crabtree Publishing Company

PMB 16A,
350 Fifth Avenue
Suite 3308
New York
N.Y. 10118

612 Welland Avenue
St. Catharines
Ontario, Canada
L2M 5V6

73 Lime Walk
Headington
Oxford OX3 7AD
United Kingdom

Cataloging in Publication Data
Kalman, Bobbie, 1947-
    Mexico. The culture / Bobbie Kalman. - Rev. ed.
    p. cm. -- (The lands, peoples, and cultures series)
    Includes index.
    ISBN 0-7787-9363-X (RLB) -- ISBN 0-7787-9731-7 (pbk)
    1. Mexico -- Civilization--Juvenile literature. [1. Mexico--Civilization.] I. Title. II. Series.

F1208.5 .K32 2002
972--dc21
2001028189
LC

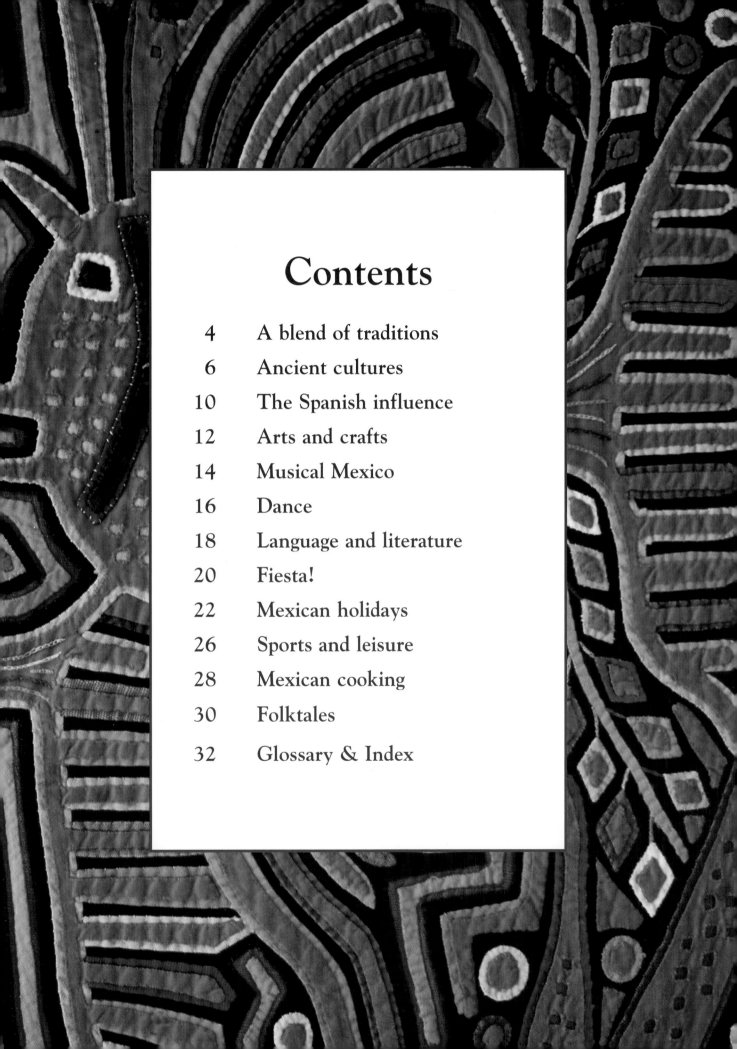

Contents

A blend of traditions

Mexico's lively culture is a mix of traditions from the past as well as more recent customs. It is also made up of the customs and traditions of different peoples. Many influences have blended over the centuries and resulted in a culture that is uniquely Mexican. *Olé!*

Back to pyramid times

Mexico's culture has ancient beginnings. It goes back to a time when native peoples built pyramids in the rainforest thousands of years ago. The native peoples of Mexico lived in advanced societies. Traces of their writings, mathematical skills, remarkable buildings, and religions are still evident in Mexico today.

More recent influences

The culture of Mexico has also been influenced by the Spanish, who sailed over from Europe, invaded, and ruled the country for many years. Among many other things, the Spanish brought their language, **architecture**, and religion to Mexico. Mexico's neighbor, the United States, has also contributed to the modern culture of Mexico through television programs, movies, music, and fashion.

(opposite page) Mexican celebrations feature colorful costumes and lively dances.

(below) These ruins reveal a Mayan city that was inhabited from 600 A.D. to 900 A.D.

Ancient cultures

About 40,000 years ago, people from Asia crossed a sandbar or an ice bridge in the **Bering Strait** to Alaska. Gradually, these people moved south through North America. By 20,000 B.C., some had migrated as far south as Mexico and Central America.

The Olmecs

The first major **civilization** in Mexico was a group of people called the Olmecs. The Olmecs flourished on the eastern coast of Mexico from about 1500 B.C. to 200 B.C. The Olmecs had complex political and religious systems, and produced many kinds of art. Later civilizations were greatly influenced by the Olmec culture.

Zapotecs and Mixtecs

Two advanced civilizations developed in the southern state of Oaxaca—the Zapotecs and the Mixtecs. The Zapotec civilization existed from about 600 B.C. to 800 A.D. Their capital city was called Monte Albán. The Zapotecs developed a system of **hieroglyphs** and wrote down their history on stone tablets. This was the first system of writing in North America.

The Mixtec civilization existed from about 800 A.D. to 1500 A.D. The Mixtecs were skilled craftspeople, and were known especially for their goldsmiths. The Mixtecs also recorded their customs and history by painting **pictograms** onto pieces of deerskin. Descendants of the Zapotecs and Mixtecs still live in Mexico today.

Teotihuacán

A city called Teotihuacán existed in central Mexico from about 200 A.D. to 900 A.D. Teotihuacán was an important religious, commercial, and political center. As many as 200,000 people lived and worked in the houses, apartments, temples, pyramids, and palaces of Teotihuacán.

The Maya

From 200 B.C. to 900 A.D., the Maya were one of the most powerful groups in Mexico. From the information that remains about this ancient culture, we know that the Mayan people had many skills. They were experts at mathematics, **astronomy**, and **astrology**, and they used a complex calendar system. Descendants of the Maya live in modern-day Mexico.

(above) The Serpent Head on the Platform of Venus and The Complex of 1000 Columns are part of the ancient site of Chichén Itzá. Most of this city was built by the Maya, although some buildings are believed to be the work of later inhabitants of the city.

(right) Statues of Mayan gods have been uncovered all across southern Mexico. Most have serious expressions on their faces, as this statue does. The elaborate headdress identifies the importance of the god.

(opposite page, inset) An Olmec stone head statue in the state of Veracruz.

(opposite page, bottom) Many native groups played a type of ball game. This Mayan ball court shows the stone ring used for scoring. Each team tried to throw the ball through the other team's ring.

Mayan facts

- The Maya had books, called codices, written with hieroglyphs. Each codex told stories about Mayan gods and important people.
- Mayan artists created large murals, or wall paintings, showing royal ceremonies.
- The Mayan civilization is famous for its elaborate buildings, which demanded great engineering skills. They built pyramids that were sometimes 200 feet (60 meters) high! The pyramids were **monuments** to Mayan gods and leaders.
- Religion was an important part of Mayan life. The Maya believed that each part of the world was ruled by a different god. The gods could bring health, good crops, and plentiful food to the people, or they could send illness and hunger.
- Mayan society was based on a class system. A person's class determined his or her job, dwelling place, and marriage partner.
- When Mayan women died, they passed their belongings on to their daughters. Mayan men passed their property down to their sons.
- At one time, experts believed that the Maya were a peaceful people. The Maya were actually a warlike people. Fights between cities were common.
- One unusual Mayan weapon was the hornet bomb—a hornet nest thrown at enemies during battle. Ouch! Nobody knows how the Maya gathered and stored these weapons without getting stung.
- The Maya also kept bees, which provided them with honey and wax.

Ancient wanderers

In the 1300s, a group of native people called the Mexica were traveling around and searching for a place to live. A message from their god Huitzilopochtli told them to look for an eagle sitting on a cactus, eating a snake. This would be a sign showing them where to build a city. When they reached Lake Texcoco, in the center of the country, the Mexica saw the sign. They built their city on an island in the lake and called it Tenochtitlán.

The Aztec people

The Mexica were also known as the Aztecs. Their culture centered around the city of Tenochtitlán from 1325 A.D. to about 1500 A.D. They formed an **alliance** with two nearby cities and eventually became the most powerful people in the country. Aztec society was made up of rulers, nobles, priests, warriors, slaves, farmers, and artisans called *tolteca*.

(right) The Aztecs are the ancestors of many present-day Mexicans. Traditional Aztec clothing shows the importance of decorative design.

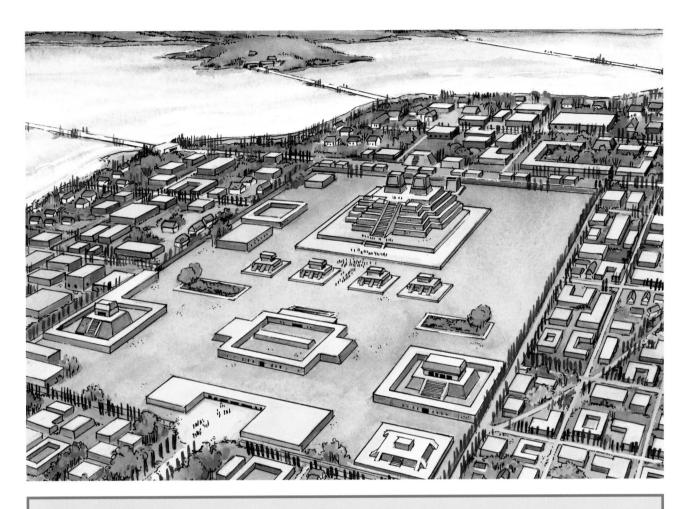

Aztec facts

• The Aztecs loved chocolate! Emperor Moctezuma often enjoyed a drink made of cocoa beans, vanilla, and chili peppers.

• Aztecs had strict laws about clothing. Most people dressed plainly, and only nobles were allowed to wear jewelry, shoes, and colorful clothing. The most important people wore garments decorated with feathers.

• The Aztec people worshiped hundreds of gods. Their main god was Huitzilopochtli, the god of war. The Aztecs performed human sacrifices as a tribute to all the gods. If they did not, they believed that the gods would be angry and the world would end.

• Creativity was important to the Aztecs, and artisans were highly respected. They brought Mayan, Zapotec, and Mixtec artists to Tenochtitlán—sometimes against their will! From these peoples, Aztecs learned the arts of **tie-dying**, **batiking**, feather-working, and **embroidery**.

(above) A sketch of the ancient city of Tenochtitlán.

(below) The huge Aztec Calendar Stone stood in the Great Temple in Tenochtitlán. This brightly painted, flat, round stone showed the Sun God surrounded by symbols that represented the stars and planets. It was used by Aztec priests to remember religious holidays and predict solar eclipses.

The Spanish influence

Spanish explorers arrived in Mexico in 1519. They wanted to claim the land for Spain, so they conquered the native peoples. The Spanish destroyed much of the native art and architecture of Mexico. The Aztec city of Tenochtitlán was torn down, and the modern capital of Mexico City was built on its ruins.

Greedy for gold

The Spanish were led by a man named Hernán Cortés. They were fascinated by the numerous golden objects they saw in Tenochtitlán. Their desire for gold was one of the reasons why they attacked the Aztecs and their city. The Spanish conquered Tenochtitlán and kept the treasure for themselves. Hungry for more gold, they enslaved many Native Mexicans and forced them to work under terrible conditions in mines. Many died while mining the gold that the Spaniards used for making jewelry, statues, and church decorations.

Devastated by disease

The Spanish explorers brought many things with them to Mexico. One of the most devastating was disease. The native peoples had no **natural resistance** to European diseases such as smallpox, measles, and tuberculosis. Millions of natives died. The native population fell from 25 million to less than two million.

Spanish language

The Spaniards had a strong influence on Mexico's language. Dozens of native languages were spoken in Mexico, but the Spaniards forced the Mexican people to learn to speak Spanish. Today some native tongues are still spoken in rural areas, but Spanish is the national language of Mexico.

(below) Before the arrival of the Spanish, many different native languages were spoken. Today, Spanish is the national language of Mexico.

Christianity

Before the Spaniards arrived, Native Mexicans worshiped many gods and practiced their own religious rituals and traditions. Spanish priests converted the native peoples to Christianity, a religion that believes in only one God. **Roman Catholicism**, which is a **denomination** of Christianity, is now the most widely practiced religion in Mexico. Native ways still remain, but they have blended with Roman Catholic traditions. For example, ancient native dances are performed to celebrate Catholic holidays.

Graceful architecture

The Spanish built hundreds of Catholic churches in Mexico. These buildings are majestic and beautiful. The town of San Miguel de Allende is proud of its handsome Spanish **colonial** architecture. It is one of three towns in Mexico that have been declared national monuments. This means that it is illegal for any of the buildings, with their graceful arches and **spires**, to be torn down.

(above) Detailed carvings and statues can be found on many Spanish colonial churches.

(bottom) The Cathedral of Guadalajara is an example of the beautiful Catholic churches that the Spanish built throughout Mexico.

Arts and crafts

Folk art

Mexican artisans have been creating beautiful handmade crafts for thousands of years. Today, many Mexican villagers carry on the ancient traditions of the Aztec *tolteca*, or artisans. The **silversmiths** of Taxco are world famous for their jewelry, and the craftsworkers of Talavera are well known for their terra cotta pottery. Artists in Jalisco have a reputation for making beautiful handblown glassware. Several villages in the Oaxacan Valley specialize in painting wooden carvings of animals, people, and other creatures.

Murals

Hundreds of years ago, the Maya painted colorful murals showing scenes of wealthy people enjoying life. The tradition of painting murals is still popular in Mexico, but modern murals present different themes, such as poverty and suffering. The most famous muralists of the twentieth century are known as "The Big Three." They are Diego Rivera, José Clemente Orozco, and David Alfaro Siqueiros. Diego Rivera painted many scenes from Mexican historical events. His colorful, realistic works revealed his strong political beliefs.

(top) Artist Diego Rivera created murals that depicted the problems faced by Mexican peasants and native peoples.

(below) Ceramics, such as this burro figurine, are popular souvenirs for visitors from other countries.

(above) Mexico is famous for its colorful textiles—whether it is clothing, rugs, blankets, or wall hangings. Some items are hand loomed in rural villages. Other pieces are mass produced in Mexico's many factories.

(above) Mexican artist Frida Kahlo lived from 1907 to 1954. She painted in a simple style called *primitivism. Kahlo's paintings are collected by art lovers around the world. This painting shows her wedding day. She was married to fellow artist Diego Rivera.*

 # Musical Mexico

Like people everywhere, Mexicans listen to all kinds of music—from rock to traditional to classical. There are eight major **symphony orchestras** in Mexico. Traditional Mexican music is still played by *mariachis* and *norteños*. Some Mexican folk songs have been around for hundreds of years, such as the popular song *La Cucaracha*, which means "the cockroach." In village **plazas**, musicians play on xylophone-like instruments called *marimbas*. The guitar has traditionally been one of the most important instruments in Mexican music.

Mariachis

For many people, *mariachi* bands are a symbol of Mexico. *Mariachis* are groups of six to eight musicians who wander around plazas and in and out of taverns and restaurants, playing songs for a fee. An average *mariachi* band has a singer, a guitar player, two violinists, two horn players, and a **bass** player. Band members dress in sparkling uniforms and wide-brimmed hats. *Mariachis* date from the short time in the 1860s that the French army occupied Mexico. Many French soldiers married Mexican women, and they hired small bands to play at their weddings. The bands were later called *mariachis*, from the French word for marriage (*mariage*). They became popular at all kinds of celebrations.

Norteños

Norteños, or *rancheros* as they are sometimes called, are not well known outside Mexico, but they are popular within the country. *Norteño* groups have three musicians: an accordion player, a guitarist, and a singer who also drums on a piece of wood with drumsticks. *Norteño* music sounds like country-and-western music. A branch of *norteño* music called *banda* developed in the 1990s. Brass instruments are played instead of guitars, and the music is a blend of Latin and traditional Mexican sounds.

María Grever

One of Mexico's favorite songwriters is a woman named María Grever. Grever wrote 873 popular songs in her lifetime! She lived from 1885 to 1951. Many of her songs were inspired by ancient Mexican folk songs. Grever was awarded the Civil Merit Medal for her cultural gift to the Mexican people.

(above) Mariachis stroll through city streets looking for someone who needs some cheerful music. Mariachi bands are also hired to play at events such as weddings and fiestas, and at hotels to entertain tourists.

Carlos Chávez

Carlos Chávez's powerful music made him the most famous classical **composer** in the history of Mexico. In 1917, Chávez wrote his first symphony, at the age of eighteen! During his long musical career, Chávez worked as a **conductor**, teacher, and director. He was responsible for the creation of the National Opera of Mexico. His goal was to remind people of the beauty of ancient native music.

Modern sounds

Today, Mexican young people listen to rock music from around the world, as well as *tejano* music. *Tejano* refers to a people and culture born in present-day Texas of Mexican heritage. *Tejano* music is a blend of polka, pop, country, and blues music. Originally, *tejano* music was ballads sung in Spanish by Mexican workers in the fields and at celebrations. The traditional instruments include a button accordion and a twelve-string guitar, called a bajo sexto. Modern-day *tejano* bands also play keyboards, saxophones, and drums.

(above) Performers such as Selena Quintanilla Perez have popularized modern-day tejano music. Tejano refers to a people and culture born in present-day Texas of Mexican heritage. Selena's Spanish-language songs made her a popular Latino star in the United States and Mexico. Since Selena's death in 1995, her music and the tejano style have become known throughout the world.

(below) Outdoor classical music concerts are partly the result of composer Carlos Chavez's lifelong devotion to classical music.

Dance

Dance is an important part of Mexican culture. Mexicans feel that it keeps them in touch with their native **heritage**. Different styles of dance are performed in each region of the country. Ancient dances are performed in traditional costumes. Modern performers base their steps on the movements of centuries-old dances.

Dance of the Little Old Men

The *danza de los viejitos*, or "Dance of the Little Old Men," is one of the oldest dances in Mexico. Young men are made up to look like toothless, wrinkled old men. The dancers hobble around with walking sticks until suddenly they leap up and start dancing energetically. Just as quickly, they become weak old men again until another burst of energy hits them. These antics cause the audience to erupt in gales of laughter.

Traveling dancers

Conchero dancers often perform at Mexican celebrations called fiestas. Men and women dance ancient native dances to the music of a guitar or lute. Their colorful costumes include tall, plumed headdresses, wide capes, sequined robes, embroidered shields, and clusters of bells and dried shells at the ankles. *Conchero* dancers travel from fiesta to fiesta, dancing for hours.

Dances with swords

Matachin sword dancers are also popular at fiestas, delighting both children and adults. The dancers wear tall, pointed headdresses and cover part of their faces with a fringe. Dressed in layers of aprons and colored ribbons, the dancers shake gourd rattles in one hand and wield brightly painted wooden swords in the other.

(left and opposite page, top) Mexican dancers perform at fiestas, tourist hotels, and night clubs.

Ballet

The Ballet Folklórico was formed by Mexican dancer Amália Hernández in 1952. Today the Folklórico has three different troupes of dancers. Two of them tour the world, and the third performs at the Palace of Fine Arts in Mexico City. The Folklórico performances combine modern dance techniques with traditional native costumes and music. Ballets are based on ancient stories of the gods and emperors. The colorful costumes and lively dance routines have gained fame in Mexico and around the world.

Mexican Hat Dance

The *jarabe tapatío*, or Mexican Hat Dance, is the national dance of Mexico. Male dancers wear a rodeo-rider costume, called a *charro*, and the women wear brightly colored full skirts that swirl around them as they move. The performers dance with quick hopping steps around a wide-brimmed Mexican hat called a sombrero.

(below) The Mexican Hat Dance is the national dance of Mexico and is sometimes performed at fiestas.

Language and literature

Spanish is the most commonly spoken language in Mexico. Over 50 native languages are still spoken by various groups of people. Until recently, many remote communities of Native Mexicans resisted learning Spanish. Now more people are learning to speak Spanish in order to find jobs and fit into the Spanish-speaking Mexican society. Today, Mexican children who grow up in native communities call the native languages "Grandma's tongue."

Mexican Spanish

Although the Spanish language was brought to Mexico by the Spanish conquerors, Mexican Spanish has developed differently than the Spanish spoken in Spain. For example, in Mexico the letter "c" is hard, like in the word "cat." In Spain, the letter "c" is pronounced like the sound "th" in English. Also, many words from native languages have been adopted into Mexican Spanish.

Pronouncing Spanish

Unlike the English language, every single letter is sounded in Spanish.

- The letter **j** is pronounced **h**. For example, the name "Juan" sounds like "hwan."
- The letter **c** is hard, as in "cat."
- The letter **z** is pronounced **th**.
- Double **l** is pronounced like the letter **y**. The Spanish word for castle, *castillo*, is pronounced "cas-TEE-yoh."
- The letter **g** is always hard, as in "go," never soft, as in "giraffe."
- When you see the letters **qu**, they are not pronounced **kw** as in "quiet." Instead, they sound like the letter **k**. The Spanish word "que," meaning "what," is pronounced "kay."
- The letter **e** at the end of words is not silent. It is pronounced "ay," as in guacamole (gwa-cah-MO-lay).

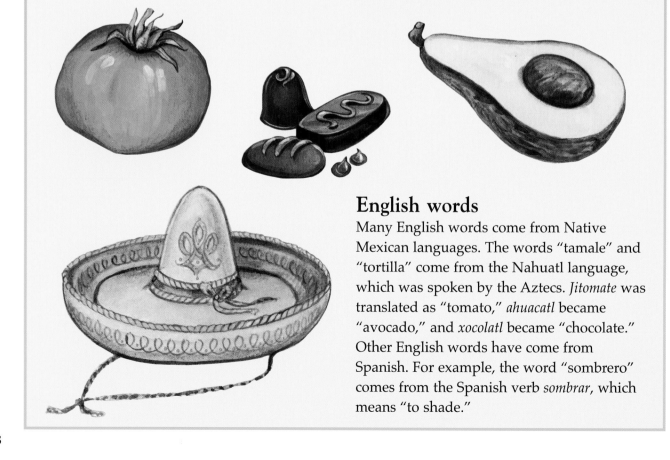

English words

Many English words come from Native Mexican languages. The words "tamale" and "tortilla" come from the Nahuatl language, which was spoken by the Aztecs. *Jitomate* was translated as "tomato," *ahuacatl* became "avocado," and *xocolatl* became "chocolate." Other English words have come from Spanish. For example, the word "sombrero" comes from the Spanish verb *sombrar*, which means "to shade."

Publishing

The first printing press in North America was used in Mexico City in 1539. Today, writing is still one of Mexico's greatest contributions to world culture. Book, newspaper, and magazine publishing are large industries in Mexico.

Literature old and new

One of the first books written about Mexico was called *The Discovery and Conquest of Mexico*. It was written by Bernal Díaz, a Spanish priest who traveled with Hernán Cortés in the 1500s. In more recent times, Mexican authors have gained recognition throughout the world. **Nobel Prize**-winning author Gabriel García Marquez lives in Mexico. He is noted for books such as *One Hundred Years of Solitude* and *Love in the Time of Cholera*. Writer Laura Esquivel produced a bestselling novel called *Like Water for Chocolate*, which showed the importance of family and food to Mexican culture. The novel now has more than three million copies in print and was made into a highly successful movie in 1992.

Poets

One of Mexico's earliest poets was a seventeenth-century **nun** named Sister Juana Inès de la Cruz. Her poetry is considered among the finest ever written in the Spanish language. Octavio Paz is a popular modern Mexican poet who has written a great deal about Mexican life. Rosario Castellanos writes poems about the native peoples of the state of Chiapas and the changing role of women in Mexican society.

(above) All subjects in Mexican schools are taught in Spanish.

(left) Several Spanish-language newspapers and magazines are published in Mexico.

 # Fiesta!

In Mexico, there are 365 main fiesta days—a holiday for every day of the year! Fiesta means "feast day" in Spanish, but feasts are only one part of these Mexican celebrations. Religious festivals, parades, fireworks, music, and dancing are other favorite ways of rejoicing.

Many reasons to celebrate

Celebrations are not limited to feast days. Weddings, graduations, birthdays, **baptisms**, **First Communions**, and **confirmations** are also festive occasions. On these days, Mexicans hire a *mariachi* band, send flowers, and invite friends and family to help celebrate. Fiestas are also held to celebrate visitors to Mexico and allow them to sample Mexico's rich culture.

Happy birthday!

Birthdays are an important cause for celebration in Mexico. In some cases, the birthdays begin early in the morning as children are woken by a *mariachi* band right outside their bedroom window! Birthday fiestas are fun-filled occasions. Family and friends gather in the house or the park for an afternoon of food and games. The highlight of the party is breaking open the *piñata* after dinner. *Piñatas* sometimes come in traditional star or horse shapes, but modern birthday *piñatas* look like popular cartoon characters.

(above) Fiesta means "feast day" in Spanish, and the celebrations often include fireworks, parades, music and dancing.

(top left) This couple will celebrate their wedding with a huge fiesta.

(top right) If this young girl can break the birthday piñata, she will find the goodies inside.

(left) Food is an important part of every fiesta. These friends enjoy ice cream cones at a birthday fiesta.

Holidays are a time of great celebration in Mexico. Some holidays are religious, such as Christmas and Easter. Others are political, such as Independence Day and Cinco de Mayo. No matter what type of holiday, you can be sure that there are fiestas in every city and town in the country on these important days.

Day of Our Lady of Guadalupe

Mexico's largest and most popular holiday celebrates the Virgin of Guadalupe. Mary, the mother of Jesus Christ, appeared in a vision to a Native Mexican man many years ago. Jesus was the founder of the Christian religion. Every year on December 12, over six million people travel to the Virgin's **shrine**, called La Villa, in Mexico City. Mexicans in other cities decorate their local plaza with flags and balloons where they gather for music and dancing. After dark, a bamboo *castillo*, or castle, is brightly lit by spectacular fireworks that explode and show the outlines of birds and flowers. No one would ever think of going home until the spectacular fireworks show is over!

Christmas

Christmas is a favorite holiday of Mexican children, perhaps because it lasts for more than one week! During the Christmas season, many Mexican families proudly display **nativity scenes** in their homes. These scenes, called *nacimientos*, contain beautifully crafted wax statues of Mary, Joseph, and the baby Jesus.

The *posada*

Christmas celebrations begin on December 16 with a *posada*, which is a play about Mary and Joseph's journey to Bethlehem before the birth of their son, Jesus Christ. *Posadas* are performed every evening until December 25. After each *posada*, there is great excitement as the children gather around a *piñata* filled with toys and candy. Wearing blindfolds, they try to break the *piñata* open with a stick.

(below) *On many days of celebration, Mexicans crowd the streets to join in parades or processions.*

Celebrating the Three Wise Men

Mexican children do not receive presents on Christmas Day. Gift-giving occurs on January 6, the day on which Mexicans celebrate the arrival of the Three Wise Men at the birthplace of Jesus. On this day, Mexican bakers busily prepare *La Rosca de los Reyes*, or the Ring of the Wise Men, a delicious circular cake with a tiny porcelain doll mixed in with the dough. The little doll represents the gifts the Wise Men gave to baby Jesus. It is a surprise for the person who finds it.

Easter

Chocolate bunnies and decorated eggs are not a part of Mexican Easter. Feasting, dancing, and merrymaking are ways in which Mexicans celebrate this Christian holiday. On the Saturday before Easter, a custom called "the Burning of Judas" takes place. In the past, effigies, or life-sized dolls, of Judas Iscariot were burned. Judas was the disciple who betrayed Jesus. Today, Mexicans burn effigies of politicians they dislike.

(above) Children get their picture taken with the Three Wise Men on January 6.

(right) Young girls dressed in white from head to toe participate in an Easter parade.

The Day of the Dead

On the first two days of November, Mexican families honor their dead relatives. This religious celebration may sound sad, but it is actually a joyful occasion. Many Mexicans believe that the spirits of their dead family members visit them during this time. Everyone goes to the cemetery to decorate family graves with flowers and gifts before enjoying a picnic nearby. The picnic is believed to make the ghosts feel welcome. At night, candles are lit at each grave to help the spirits find their resting places in the darkness.

The Day of the Dead is a time of remembering loved ones, and it is a time of festivity. Mexican children look forward to eating candies and suckers in the shape of human skulls. Mexican bakers try to outdo one another by baking the most delicious coffee cake, called *Pan de los Muertos*, or Bread of the Dead.

(opposite page) A mock wedding for skeletons is a fun part of Day of the Dead celebrations.

(below) This family sits by a relative's grave on the evening of November 1. Offerings of flowers, food, and candles make the ghosts of dead relatives feel welcome.

Cinco de Mayo

Cinco de Mayo, or the Fifth of May, is a celebration of a battle that took place in the town of Puebla. In 1862, a small Mexican army, led by Benito Juárez, defeated French troops who were trying to take over the country. Large Cinco de Mayo festivities take place every year in Puebla, which is now a large city. Mexicans all over the country celebrate this holiday as a symbol of their freedom and independence.

Independence Day

Independence Day festivities are held on September 16. Mexicans celebrate the fact that their country claimed independence from Spain on this day in 1821. Flags, noise makers, confetti, and Mexico's official colors of red, white, and green can be seen on this holiday. Cries of "Long Live Mexico!" can be heard throughout the crowds of people who gather to rejoice on Independence Day.

Benito Juárez's birthday

March 21 is a national holiday held in honor of the birthday of Benito Juárez. Juárez was the first Native Mexican to become president of the country. During his fourteen years as president, Juárez worked to protect the rights of the Mexican people. Today, Mexicans think of him as a national hero.

Day of Saint Anthony the Abbot

January 17 is a special day for Mexican children—and for their pets, too! On this day, which honors the saint who loved children and animals, young people wash and brush their pets and sometimes even dress them in decorated collars and fancy hats! In the morning, the children and animals form a long line and parade through the town and into the churchyard, where the local priest waits to bless the animals one by one. In the city, boys and girls bring cats, dogs, turtles, or goldfish, whereas country children bring chickens, ducks, sheep, or **burros**. No animal is too big or too small to be blessed!

Sports and leisure

In their spare time, Mexicans like to do activities such as exercise, watch television and movies, visit friends and family, read, or play games and sports. Some of the sports that Mexican citizens enjoy are soccer, baseball, basketball, boxing, tennis, and golf.

Fútbol

Fútbol, called soccer in the United States and Canada, is the most popular sport in Mexico. The country has a professional soccer league in which dozens of teams compete. Important games are played in the Azteca Stadium in Mexico City. This huge stadium can hold up to 100,000 people. The World Cup, the most popular soccer championship in the world, takes place every four years. When Mexico competes in the World Cup, everyone follows the matches on television or radio, hoping that the Mexican national team will win.

Béisbol

Béisbol, or baseball, is almost as popular as soccer. It was introduced to Mexico by the United States over 50 years ago. Since then, many famous baseball players have come from Mexico, including Bobby Avila, who played with the Cleveland Indians in the 1950s. After he retired from baseball, he became an important politician. He is a national hero.

Jai alai

Jai alai, or *pelota*, is a fast-paced Spanish game played with a hard rubber ball and a wicker bat, called a *cesta*, which is tied to the player's wrist. *Jai alai* is a little bit like tennis, but it is much faster. Some people call it the fastest ball game in the world because the ball can travel up to 160 miles (260 kilometers) per hour!

Handball

Balonmano, or handball, is one of the world's oldest pastimes. It is especially popular among Mexican boys and girls. The Maya of ancient Mexico had handball courts that can still be seen among the ancient ruins. Their version of handball was not just a game but a religious ceremony. The ball represented the sun, which was considered a powerful god. If a person was unlucky enough to drop the ball, he or she had to die. Today, handball is less dangerous to people's health. It is played just for fun!

Rodeos

Most Mexican towns have a rodeo ring where riders, called *charros*, perform tricks on horseback and rope bulls with lassoes. These popular rodeos, called *charreodas*, are followed by lively parties.

(right) This young boy proudly shows off the tight costume and wide-brimmed sombrero of the charro.

The bullfighting tradition

The Spanish conquerors brought bullfighting to Mexico in the sixteenth century. It is still a popular spectator sport, especially for visitors. There are over 220 bullrings in Mexico, where bullfighting takes place from November to April. The Plaza México bullring, located in Mexico City, is the largest in the world.

Matadors

Expert bullfighters are called matadors. Being a matador is dangerous. Many are crippled and even killed during a bullfight. While fighting the bull, the matador waves a bright red cape. It was once believed that the color red makes bulls angry, but bulls are colorblind. It is the movement of the cape that angers the bulls. The best matadors are admired for their bravery and are considered heroes. When a matador kills a bull honorably, the cry *"Olé!"* is heard throughout the bullring.

Cruelty to animals

Some people think that bullfighting is an act of cruelty to animals. During a bullfight, the bull is stabbed in the shoulders and then stung with barbed sticks. Wounded and bleeding, the bull becomes angry and charges the matador. The matador must then kill the bull with a sword. Other people see bullfighting as an artform. Many Mexicans consider bullfighting an important part of their culture and believe that it is no more cruel than killing other animals for their meat.

(below) Bullfighting was introduced to Mexico by the Spanish. It is a dangerous sport that draws thousands of visitors to Mexico each year.

Mexican cooking

Mexican food is a flavorful mix of Spanish and native cooking. Long before such foods as tomatoes, corn, avocados, vanilla, and cocoa were eaten in other parts of the world, cooks in ancient Mexico were using them in a wide variety of dishes. When the Spanish arrived in the 1500s, they introduced new foods, spices, and cooking techniques to the native peoples. Pork, dairy products, and citrus fruits were quickly accepted into the Mexican diet. Today, Mexican food differs from region to region. In some areas it is hot and spicy; in others it is rich and sweet.

Making a Mexican meal

Invite your family to eat an authentic Mexican meal prepared by you! Making tacos, guacamole, Mexican hot chocolate, and polvorones is easy! Be sure to ask an adult for help when using a knife or the stove.

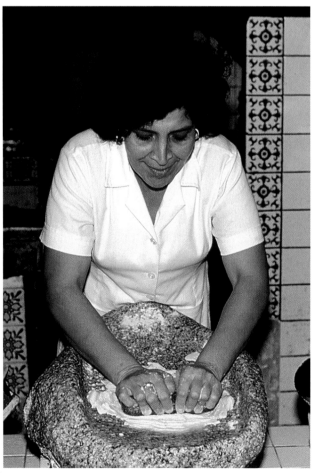

Tacos

Corn is the most important staple food in Mexico. A staple food is one that is eaten every day. Corn is nutritious and is used in almost every dish, including tamales, enchiladas, and tortillas. Tacos are tortillas that are filled with a variety of vegetable, cheese, bean, or meat fillings. They are as popular in Mexico as hamburgers are in the United States. You can make them at home using this recipe.

1 lb (450 g) ground chicken or hamburger
1 teaspoon (5 ml) Mexican seasoning
1 teaspoon (5 ml) onion flakes
1 teaspoon (5 ml) dried cilantro
dash of cumin
dash of cayenne
12 taco shells
12 oz (340 g) shredded cheese
2 tomatoes
1 avocado
1 small head of lettuce

Brown meat in a frying pan. Drain excess grease. Add Mexican seasoning, onion flakes, cilantro, cumin, and cayenne. Cover and simmer for ten minutes.

Chop tomatoes and peeled avocado into small pieces. Shred the lettuce with hands or a knife. Place these toppings on separate plates. Heat taco shells in 300°F (150°C) oven for five minutes. Fill them with meat mixture. Top with tomatoes, avocado, lettuce, and cheese. This recipe makes twelve tacos.

(left) This woman is making tortillas, a staple food in the Mexican diet.

Guacamole

Guacamole is a favorite dip in some parts of Mexico. Serve guacamole with corn chips as an appetizer. Leftover guacamole can be stored in an airtight container in the refrigerator. Put the avocado pit in the middle of the dip—it helps keep the guacamole fresh!

2 ripe avocados
1/2 small onion
2 tomatoes
1 jalapeño pepper (optional)
2 tablespoons (30 ml) lemon juice
2-3 sprigs fresh cilantro (optional)
salt and pepper

Peel avocados and mash with fork. Place in bowl. Chop onion, cilantro, and pepper finely. Peel tomatoes and chop finely. Put all chopped ingredients in bowl. Add lemon juice, salt, and pepper to taste. Mix well. If you are not serving right away, cover bowl tightly with plastic wrap or foil, then refrigerate.

Mexican hot chocolate

Long ago the Aztecs prepared a royal drink called *chocolatl*, which was made with cocoa beans and chilies! The Spanish developed a new version of the drink by taking out the chilies and adding sugar and cinnamon. The result is a delicious frothy concoction that is easy to make.

2 oz (60 ml) unsweetened chocolate
2 cups (500 ml) milk
1 cup (250 ml) heavy cream
6 tablespoons (90 ml) sugar
dash of cinnamon

Melt chocolate in the top of a double boiler. In a separate pot, warm milk and cream on low heat until hot but not boiling. Add a little hot milk to melted chocolate to form a paste. Stir in remaining milk, cream, sugar, and cinnamon. Serve immediately and enjoy!

(top) Snack time! Street vendors set up stands in busy plazas and marketplaces and sell many kinds of Mexican food.

Polvorones

Polvorones are Mexican sugar cookies. They go well with hot chocolate.

2 cups (500 ml) flour
3/4 cup (180 ml) sugar
1/2 teaspoon (2.5 ml) cinnamon
1 cup (250 ml) butter or margarine
extra sugar and cinnamon

Preheat oven to 300°F (150°C). Sift together flour, cinnamon, and sugar. Cream butter with beater. Gradually add flour mixture. Pinch off small pieces of dough and shape into 24 patties. Place on ungreased cookie sheet. Bake for 25 minutes. Sprinkle extra sugar and cinnamon over warm cookies.

Folktales

Folktales and legends

Mexican folktales, or myths, spring from several sources. Some come from the Mayan people, some from the Aztecs, and others are a combination of many native cultures. The following legend tells the story of the creation of the earth. It explains how people came to be.

The five suns

The ancient Aztecs believed that the gods tried to create the earth four times. Each time, something went wrong. On the fifth try, everything worked and that is the age that we are living in today. Here's what happened:

On the first try, a god named Tezcatlipoca turned himself into the sun. Giants lived on the earth. They ate acorns, berries, and roots. The god Quetzalcoatl became jealous that Tezcatlipoca was ruling the universe, and he knocked Tezcatlipoca out of the sky. Tezcatlipoca was so angry that he turned into a jaguar and destroyed the giants and the earth.

During the second age, Quetzalcoatl took over the heavens. He created humans, and they ate pine nuts. Tezcatlipoca got his revenge by overthrowing Quetzalcoatl and destroying the earth with a hurricane. A few humans were left, and they were transformed into monkeys.

The third age began when Tlaloc, the god of rain, became the sun. Humans populated the earth once again. The age ended when the earth was destroyed by fire. The humans who survived were turned into dogs, turkeys, birds, and butterflies.

On the fourth try, the water goddess Chalchiuhtlicue became the sun. This time, the earth was destroyed by a great flood. The humans who survived were turned into fish.

The fifth and final age occurred after the gods held a meeting and decided that one of them had to sacrifice him or herself to become the new sun by jumping into a fire. A god named Tecuciztecatl was chosen, but he was too afraid to sacrifice himself. A goddess named Nanahuatzin was then chosen, and she bravely jumped into the fire and became the sun. Tecuciztecatl was embarrassed that Nanahuatzin had done something that he could not, so he followed her into the fire. He was too late to become the sun, and became the moon instead. Quetzalcoatl then created humankind, and we are the people who live on earth today!

Glossary

alliance A partnership agreement between two or more individuals or groups

architecture The design and construction of buildings and structures

astrology The belief that the position of planets and stars affect people's lives

astronomy The study of the planets and stars

baptism A ceremony that shows that a person has become a Christian

bass A large violin-like instrument that plays low notes

batik A method of dying cloth to create interesting designs

Bering Strait A channel of water that separates northeast Asia from northwest North America

burro A small donkey

civilization A society with a well-established culture that has existed for a long period of time

colonial Describing a land or people ruled by a distant country

communion A Christian ceremony that remembers the death of Jesus Christ

composer A person who writes original music

conductor The person who directs a musical performance

confirmation A Christian ceremony in which a person renews his or her faith and is accepted into full membership of the church

denomination A religious group within a faith

embroidery The art of decorating cloth with needlework

First Communion A Roman Catholic celebration that occurs when a child attends his or her first communion service

heritage Traditions and beliefs passed down by previous generations

hieroglyph A picture that represents a word or sound

monument A structure that honors the memory of a person, idea, or event

myth A traditional story that tells the beliefs of a group of people

nativity scene A representation of the birthplace of Jesus Christ

natural resistance The human body's ability to defend against illness and disease

Nobel Prize An international prize awarded for achievements in areas such as science, literature, and peace

novelist A person who writes novels, or books

nun A woman who has devoted her life to God

pictogram A drawing or picture that represents information

piñata A hollow, treat-filled papier-mâché figure broken during some Mexican celebrations

plaza An open area in the middle of a town or city

Roman Catholicism A branch of Christianity that is headed by the pope

shrine A holy site dedicated to the worship of a religious figure

silversmith An artisan who works with silver

spire A structure, such as a steeple, that comes to a point at the top

symphony orchestra A large group of musicians who play classical music

terra cotta A hard clay used for pottery

tie-dye A method of dying cloth in which parts of the fabric are knotted, creating unusual color patterns

 # Index

2 3 4 5 6 7 8 9 0   Printed in U.S.A.   2 1 0 9 8 7 6 5 4 3